EVENING TIDE

MEDITATIONS BY

ELIZABETH TARBOX

With many thanks
for your support of Unitarian Universalism
from
Friends of the UUA

Boston
Skinner House Books

*The Unitarian Universalist Association of Congregations
25 Beacon Street, Boston, MA 02108*

Thanks to Brenda Wong, Project Editor,
for her skill and patience.

Cover and text design by Suzanne Morgan.
Cover photo by Christine Wilson.

Published by Skinner House Books,
an imprint of the Unitarian Universalist Association,
25 Beacon Street,
Boston, MA 02108-2800.

Printed in the USA.

10 9 8 7 6 5 4 3 2 1
02 01 00 99 98

Library of Congress Cataloging-in-Publication Data

Tarbox, Elizabeth, 1944–
Evening Tide : meditations / by Elizabeth Tarbox.
p.   cm.
ISBN 1-55896-364-2 (alk. paper)
1. Meditations. 2. Spiritual life—Unitarian Universalist
churches. 3. Unitarian Universalist churches. I. Title.
BX9855.T37   1998
242—dc21   97-32825
                                        CIP

To the members and friends
of the Unitarian Universalist Society
of Middleborough
and the First Parish in Cohasset,
with gratitude for their gifts to me.

CONTENTS

REBIRTH

When the day is too bright, or the night too dark, and your feelings are like an avalanche barreling down the mountain of events outside your control, when you look down and you are falling and you cannot see the bottom, or when your pain has eaten you and you are nothing but an empty hungry hole, then there is an opportunity for giving.

Don't stay home and cover your head with a pillow. Go outside and plant a tulip bulb in the ground: that is an act of rebirth. Sprinkle breadcrumbs for the squirrels or sunflower seed for the birds: that is a claiming of life. And when you have done that, or if you cannot do that, go stare at a tree whose leaves are letting go for its very survival. Pick up a leaf, stare at it; it is life, it has something to teach you.

You are as precious as the birds or the tulips or the tree whose crenelated bark protects the insects who seek its shelter. You are an amazing, complex being, with poetry in your arteries, and charity layered beneath your skin. You have before you a day full of opportunities for living and giving. Do not think you know all there is to know about yourself, for you have not given enough away yet to be able to claim self-knowledge. Do you have work to do today? Then do it as if your life were hanging in the balance, do it as fiercely as if it mattered, for it does. Do you think the world doesn't need you? Think again! You cleanse the world with your breathing, you beautify the world with your giving, you perfect the world with your thinking and acting and caring.

Don't stay home and suffocate on your sorrow: go outside and give yourself to the world's asking.

PAS DE DEUX

My morning walk takes me alongside Monponsett Pond. The ways of the pond are new to me, the mist that curls over the surface and is swept up by the first strong tongue of sunlight, the dozen shades of grey the pond wears according to the season and time of day.

But the greatest gifts of this pond and my morning walks are two blue herons. The herons fly over the pond, not a foot above it, so the tips of their wings, in performance art, kiss the sealed surface without breaking it. Their reflections fly beneath them, rhythm without melody, feathered beauty lifting my soul through the day.

This is a reminder: if life finds you flying without the grace of a blue heron, let your spirit breathe each day, find a moment in your morning for the healing power of beauty and the expression of gratitude.

PRAYER FOR COMPASSION

Spirit of Life, I give thanks for the opportunities to love that present themselves in the turmoil of life.

Where the light catches the tears in another's eyes, where hands are held and there are moments without words, let us be present then, and alive to the possibility of changing. Let us seek to make another's well-being the object of our concern. Let us seek to be present to another's pain, to bathe another's wounds, hear another's sadness, celebrate another's success, and allow the other's story to change our own.

Let us stand in the morning on damp grass, hear the syllables of bird song, and fill up on sweet air that rolls over oceans and continents. Let us look up at the stars and the planets that fill the night sky with majesty. Let us witness the first fresh buds of spring amid the brown sticks of winter. And for all this, let us be grateful.

Let us not defend ourselves against the discomfort of unruly emotion, nor seek to close down our hearts for fear a new love will come to shake our foundations. Let us instead be open to discovering a new way of seeing an old problem, or appreciating the perfection of a seashell, or the possibility of friendship. For in giving ourselves to what we do not understand, we receive life's blessings, and in taking care of another, we are cared for.

HOMECOMING

I returned at sunrise to my special beach at Shipyard Lane, where morning is a soft line on the horizon and the trees have been touched by the fastidious brush of spring. And I walked slowly to the edge of the sweet ocean that moves and calls me, and I dipped my fingers in her hair and tasted the salt and knew I was home.

I want to bring you the warm smell of spring there; re-create for you the twist of a certain old wild apple tree with branches frosted with blossom, or hum the song of the chorale that sounds from every branch. I want you to place your bare feet down on that cool sand, and draw your breath deep into your own secret inner world where your truth and only your truth is spoken.

I want to press your hands lightly to the smooth grey rocks and show you the chipmunks that make their home between the rocks and the beach plum bushes. But if that cannot be, if you and I are too far apart, or don't even know each other's names, then know at least that Shipyard Lane gives me more love than I can use, plenty enough to share. And I would share it with you.

GOOD FRIDAY

I was working with a group of young people at a Safe Schools conference in Boston. They were discussing how to tell their parents they were gay or lesbian. Many of them had suffered harassment, brutality, and ostracism by their peers, and they worried about how to protect their parents from the sadness that often results from learning one's son or daughter is homosexual.

"Tell them you will always love them, even if they reject you," suggested one man.

"Talk to siblings first, ask for their support," advised another.

"It's rough," admitted a young woman, "but you stand to have a closer, more honest relationship with them once they know."

One young man had tears in his eyes. "I'm scared of hurting them," he admitted. "I never wanted to lie to them. My parents are neat people, but I'm afraid they will be so disappointed in me."

Good Friday is coming up. In our tradition, we focus more on the renewal and celebration of life than on the grief of death. Yet we cannot overlook the meaning of Good Friday in our eagerness to get to Easter morning, for death is always part of life, and sorrow is not to be avoided if we are to fully experience joy. The Christian tradition remembers the suffering of Jesus on Good Friday, and one of his concerns as he was crucified was for his mother. I looked at these fine young men and women around the table at the conference and I thought of Jesus saying, "Woman, behold your son," and to the disciple, "Behold your mother."

Like Jesus, these young men and women wanted to protect their parents from sadness and disappointment. In the Bible story, Jesus' mother stayed with him right to the end. When everyone else turned away, his mother was there. I hope this will be true too for the students I met at the conference; I hope their parents will not turn away when they are most needed. If I could speak to each one of their parents, I would say, "Behold your child, and be very proud."

EASTER

The ducks came again this year. I like to think it is nature's way of making amends for the spring rain that floods our yard.

It is a gift for Easter.

When the fruit trees start to sneeze and the pile of snow thrown from impatient shovels melts down, the mallards come and make of our yard a sanctuary. They swim about and learn soon enough that this is a temporary pond, that it is too close to the highway for raising young, that there are energetic, impolite dogs in the neighborhood who see everything as a sporting event. The ducks know they cannot stay. But for a week or two they are there in the morning when we shuffle out with our bread offering; they swim with grace through the tall grass still showing above the water; they fly up suddenly and make our yard seem like a primordial lake from which the very birth of life has sprung.

And then they leave. Yesterday, I watched as the ducks made a turn about the diminishing pond, then took off with a whooshing of wings, freed from the clasp of gravity, and flew around above my head while I murmured: please stay a little while.

Easter is an exercise in letting go. It is a reminder that life is precious and fragile, beautiful and impermanent. It is a reminder that love is a gift of immense proportions, that if we have shared it for even so fleeting a moment as the time it takes for a pair of mallards to sanctify our pond, or dawn to come to a grieving woman who watches by a tomb, then love has touched us and we will never be the same again.

BAY ROAD

The tide is high now. Through the wintering sticks of next year's hedge, I can see the marsh move above the restless motion that circles the earth and disturbs the sunlight. Outside my sliding glass door a tree full of brown sparrows earns the appellation "thickly settled." The sparrows and pink-fronted finches scrabble for their places on the three feeders, until a jay comes along and unbalances them all. So close, only a glass wall to keep them from coming in the house, or me from reaching into their tree. But our friendship is based on respect, and they are as little likely to enter my space, as I theirs.

I shall leave this place soon and do not know when I shall again live as aqueous a life. I have woken to the laughing call of seabirds and slept to the gentle reassurance of the siren on the Gurnet Lighthouse nearby. I have stroked lightly through the ripple of moonbeams across the bay at midnight and fingered the old weathered wood of the rickety dock. I am filled with this beauty, and I have to trust that the filling will last. For the world is a broken place, and I need to remember the irresistible force of water and the way it moves forward to cover the cracks just a little at a time, and the easygoing flexibility of the little dock that weathers all storms. And it is a brave world, too, full of adventure for those who do not hold on tight to the moorings, or close their eyes to the beckon of morning.

I promise not to forget. I promise that in mornings to come, though I stare from another window, I shall remember the view from this one. In warm, summer afternoons, I shall picture the water lapping against the steps and the movement of mini ice floes in the winter. I shall feed other birds and hear other comforting sounds, but I shall not forget this place and the love it has shown to my soul.

MOVING DAY

The day I moved from the beach I took a last walk along the spray-soaked pier.

The dawn came softly to Captain's Hill, and the birds overlooked my tears.

I felt other losses, which ones I cannot say; just memories, blunted now, no longer drawing blood, but wrapped like philo dough around the place I call my soul.

I need these times, though I'd just as soon avoid them. I need them to teach me things about myself I'd rather never know. These are the growing times, when I push myself to loosen the knots that tie me to old agonies and bad habits, to strengthen worn loyalties, and to find new paths to walk.

I took one last walk along the wooden pier. The tide was coming in. I'll not forget the way it looked that day.

CAT CALLING

The cat entered our lives with her tail up and her eyes alert for possibility, stalking her calling in our home, in our chairs, up the chimney, in every closet, and behind every impossible obstruction.

She stares with magic eyes, inscrutable, all-knowing. She is all cat: stealthy as a winter breeze that skims the top of the snow bank, impertinent as the sudden blast that blows smoke down the chimney and out into the room.

She seduces, lying back in our arms with the wanton abandon of Aphrodite. She exhorts, rumbling like an old volcano or yowling like an exorcised poltergeist.

I am seduced by her unabashed affection, mystified by her eyes which steal my secrets, envious of her unquestioning delight in the warmth of an armchair. It is serious, this partnership between the cat who stalks her calling and we who are called. I am in the presence of Isis, our home is her temple, and we are called to serve.

GALE FORCE

Nothing I could imagine, no weather-driven fantasy could quell the thrill of this storm. The cat and I paced about indoors until we could resist no longer. We opened the door, staggered against the wind along the dock, heard the waves cracking and spraying, and smelled the marsh's perfume. Ducks flew into the air and the wind carried them backwards. Smaller birds skimmed the surface and seemed able to move beneath the howling draft. I wondered how it would feel to be blown off this dock and dropped into the marsh grass. I was keenly aware of the neutrality of the dock. Its last six feet already had blown askew, wrenched from the piles and wedged under the remaining boards. A dock that would let go its own would soon dispose of me.

I thought of Thoreau wanting to suck out all the marrow of life, to know it fully. I wasn't fearful or anxious. I was awake, caught up in the deeper call of *Ruah*, the spirit wind, the breath of God that roars over the bay and through my bones. I wanted to be reduced to my lowest terms, my simplest elements: salt water and a few minerals, with nothing to hide. My skin contains me, but just barely. This morning I wanted to dissolve into the roaring wind, no longer standing in opposition to the elements, but becoming one with them.

THE TEACHING BEAN

When I was a child my stepmother gave me and my sister each a lima bean. She showed us how to dampen some blotting paper and line a jam jar with it, and how to place the bean carefully between the blotting paper and the jar. She told us to stand the jars on the windowsill in our bedroom and keep the blotting paper wet, and watch to see what would happen.

A little later I took my bean out and polished it up with a bit of furniture polish. It was all shiny now and smelled much better than my sister's bean.

In a few days my sister's bean swelled and a strong white root pushed out of the bottom of the bean. My bean just sat there. A week later my sister's bean sprouted a green shoot that forced its way up and out of the top of the jar. My bean did nothing, but began to look wrinkly. In another week my sister's jar was full of roots and shoots and the bean was ready to be planted. My bean shriveled up and fell to the bottom of the jar and I threw it away.

How often have I covered things with furniture polish to make them shiny, to make them smell better? How often in my life have I cared more about the way things looked, and how they smelled, rather than how they really were? I spent half a lifetime covering my feelings with the emotional equivalent of furniture polish, thinking that if I looked good and smelled good the ache inside would go away.

But spirits are not like beans, thank god. They may shrivel with neglect, but as long as life persists there is the chance to wash off the polish and redeem the growing thing inside.

PENITENT'S PRAYER

It is an hour before sunrise. The waves keep coming, but each minute they make less progress than the minute before. As the tide goes out, the beach is exposed—a million pebbles just visible in the lifting of night, a periwinkle clinging to a rock, a horseshoe crab scrambling to catch the receding ocean—and I am exposed in all my hurts and frailties. My composure drains away with the tide, and the disheveled beach mirrors the ragged edges of my soul. The whole bay is my confessional, the breath of dawn my confessor.

I have been so consumed with my own hurts that I've forgotten to call a friend whose hurt is equal to my own. I put off doing those things that might bring healing to someone who is broken, or joy to someone who is sad, or compassion to someone who is at odds with the rhythm of life, because I cared more for my own loneliness. I refused the hand of one who reached out to me, clinging instead to old familiar ways. I chose to remain stuck inside a problem, rather than ask for help to solve it.

I pray that some benevolent spirit has listened to my heart's despair and judged me not. At the edge of the clouds a rim of cream appears. Night creeps away with my guilt beneath its cloak. Dawn sprinkles absolution, the earth has kept its promise. Forgiveness is at hand.

MEDITATION FOR MOTHER'S DAY

I stood out at the low-tide mark early in the morning, and looked back at the shore a quarter of a mile away. Trees whose every branch I know when I am standing beneath them blended with their neighbors, and I could not recognize them. I found myself looking at small segments of the shore and wondering: if a sliver was all I could see, would I know it to be my beach in the morning light? Or would I know it only if I could see it all, in one majestic arc of familiar landscape? Do I know it well enough so when I cannot see it, it is still there in my memory, fresh and sweet? Is it always available in the parts of my being that cannot be left behind?

Do I know you well enough, so that I would recognize you from a great distance, from the tilt of your head, the sway of your step, or the merest whisper of your voice? Have I looked carefully at you, and noted the texture of your skin and the color of your eyes, so that when you are miles from here, I can see you easily in the space reserved for the most precious memories?

Have I trusted you enough, so you know who you are, and can be sure of yourself in a world that doesn't want to trust? Have I modeled the life I want you to live, one of caring and appreciation and feelings and love? And have I learned all I can from you, so I can draw on your wisdom and lean on your truth, even when we are far apart?

And have I loved you enough, so that you will know you are loved when the storms beat you down, the friendships disappoint, or the demands of a world that needs your love weigh too heavily on your shoulders?

Have I said thank you to the creative spirit who brought our lives close enough to touch, and who gave us the chance to notice one another and dwell together in this moment?

Then let me give thanks now.

EMBERS TO ASHES

After hearing that my father was dying in England, I went to the beach to give myself space to breathe in the truth of what was happening. There I found two horseshoe crabs dying in the dry sand, left behind by the tide. I carried them back into the water and watched them nuzzle beneath the shallow waves. And I thought my father would approve if he knew I had saved the lives of two creatures on the morning that he was dying. But I had to accept that he would never know I had been to the beach that day, and that he and I would never share another story.

When I finally arrived at the hospital, my father could not speak. He was lying neatly with a fan to keep him cool and a sheet covering the lower half of his body. My father had been a blacksmith, spending much of his life hammering red-hot iron into pleasing shapes. He would come home with dirt under his nails and sweat on his body, and his shoulder and neck muscles stood out sinewy and uneven as he washed himself at the kitchen sink. He didn't look that different to me now in the hospital bed, the same muscular shoulders and neck, the same sweat. But this blacksmith who had swung a sledgehammer over his head as if it were nothing at all, had not the strength to lift his head off the pillow. I knew he recognized me because he winked at me in the way that he would, his eyes cried as he moved his hands to invite my embrace, and it was painful to notice his helplessness.

Why would I ever have imagined that he would live forever? I had mistaken him for the pieces of his iron work—the gates and wrought iron railings around the cathedral, the fancy candle holders, the supporting iron brackets on the corners of historic buildings that will be there years after this generation has passed away. Why had I ever allowed myself to believe that he was untouchable by age when, in fact, the eighty-four years of his life had been but a blink in the scheme of things, a few moments of sunlight, the trill of a songbird on the wooden fence, the strike of a hammer on an anvil in a blacksmith's shop.

We are forged by the unrelenting blows of living that hammer us into pleasing shapes and make us unique. The bellows that startle the fire to new life are blowing behind us to keep us moving, and creation will make us useful so that when our lives have passed into the flame, there will be some part of us that will live on to support the feet of the next generation.

If you can, hold your father in your arms and look hard at his face to remember it. If that is not possible, then take some time to feel whatever it is that the thought of him evokes in you. For whatever the relationship is or has been, your father has left an imprint on you that is there for the whole of your life. Know it, honor it, and be at peace.

NOSTALGIA ON THE 5:42

Today, riding in a train from Chester to London, I passed through Berkhamsted, Hertfordshire, where I used to live. Five years we lived there before we emigrated. Five years of playing house and getting the hang of being married, shopping for furniture, sewing drapes, making coffee in the kind of elaborate glass contraption that only newly married people have, counting cash to pay the bills. I lived in Berkhamsted and worked there, too. It was the frame around my life. And here I was riding through its train station without stopping, and it didn't mind my passing, nor see my tears.

I wish I could relate my thoughts correctly instead of detaching a thread at a time (frayed here and there), a ligament, a choice, a priority. When I say "I used to live there" it reduces that fact to history, to a time only half-remembered, only ten percent important. But that is not true!

Those years were lived a day, an hour at a time, just as these days, these hours. "A long time ago" seems to give us permission to select only the choicest drama for memory's stage, the best one or two photos for the album. But that is not how it is!

We should attend to the ordinariness of our days, and remember that they imprint our spirits, line our eyes, weary our hearts, stimulate our memories, callous our hands, and make whole our lives.

SANGRE DE CRISTO

My names for god don't work here in the desert because they are ocean words. I know how to stir the mystery of the dark waters and move the spirit of briny swells to life because it is my spirit, my mother that rises from the waves to meet my call. And I am not afraid.

But here I need a new language, a language that loves clean white branches reaching to a blue sky and the hard open mouth of a dry riverbed beneath the canyon wall. Who are these gods that strike the blood-red walls of the Sangre de Cristo Mountains, where spruce and aspen with crooked fingers clutch the wild wind's laugh?

I am ill at ease out here where ravens fly upside down, huge feet curled with the ecstasy of high flight, preening their feathers in casual command of the wind's army. I can imagine being caught by a hawk's beak, carried to 10,000 feet, and being indigestible, dropped upon the desert floor. I can imagine thirst draining my veins, withering my skin till it flakes away. And I am less than I have ever been, because I do not know how to call the spirit of the mountain, or how to name the gods that move among these rocks.

Kindly, the universe puts its great lips to my ear and whispers, listen. Listen. You do not need to know the name of god, or call it. You need only to know that you do not know, and lift your face and stand in its presence and give thanks.

A NEW MEXICO EDUCATION

The red rocks won't let my eyes alone. Drawn into their hard clear lines, stark against the sky, my small self is made even smaller.

Standing beneath its silence I am afraid of being crushed by this mountain. At its crest I am afraid of falling. Neither of those things is going to happen, so it is something else, this spasm in my stomach. As I stare into the rock, notice the spruce standing tall at the mesa top, roots going god-knows-how-deep into the volcanic tuff of this mountain, I am immobilized by my insignificance. That's it. I am nothing. I am nothing to this mountain, to that tree, except as I die and add my dust to the scant topsoil between the crevices.

Self-delusion is the universal human trap. We believe in our importance and reinforce that hour by hour, in our loveless use of the earth, and especially in our religion. We have raised ourselves to the potency of mountains and tell each other it is God's plan.

But the truth is, this mountain is big. It is enduring. If God has a plan, it surely includes this mountain. And we are small, and lie to one another about our size to keep from feeling afraid.

As I stare and reflect and face the truth, I am released from my need to be noticed. I can stare at this mountain and see that it is beautiful, and I can take this beauty into myself and it will fill me up.

PINE FOREST FUGUE

The wind sings four-part harmony: aspen, piñon, ponderosa, and spruce.

What a language this is: beyond the reach of words, whispered secrets understood only at the place where the lover sighs and cries, and brings a truer life to life.

I listened at midday to the song humming over these tall, green organ pipes and I listened at dusk when the hills were rust and the sky pink with sunset. And I heard it again, the theme of a thousand pines. But I did not understand, and the chill I felt was of one who waits outside.

The raven understood, with outstretched fingers and the air between its toes, but I only closed my eyes and tried too hard to hear. I woke next morning from my bed on the forest floor, as if the hum had stroked my bones and calmed the fractious poet. And I learned to trust that my soul knows things I'll never find the words to tell, and my heart will sing to meet the forest's call.

MORNING IN ZUNI

I had quite forgotten how to pray so far from home, away from the sacristy of sea and shore, but then I watched a boy chopping wood. He swung his axe easily, slicing the piñon logs that were twisted and bent like the hieroglyphs of an ancient language.

The slopes behind the boy were buttered with sagebrush and sunrise, and his face was shining with morning chores. And for a few precious moments, I stood at his altar and caught the dimensions of his cathedral.

REVERIE ON AN AUGUST AFTERNOON

With tired feet I scrunch the pebbles at the shoreline,
walking hard, pushing my body at the wind as if I could
break through the choices and enter the place of peace.
A long tree trunk, white with ocean washing, soft with
the long slow tempering of time, beckons my body and
I sit, then lie along its narrow surface.

And from that prone and precarious balance, I see a tree
whose fruit, above the picking line, waits for autumn
winds to gather.

I see a hedge of foxglove and blueberry, queen anne's
lace and ragwort, audience to the butterfly ballet cho-
reographed by the unseen master of the dance.

I hear the triumph song of crickets and the satin swish
of ocean-tumbled pebbles and my heart reminds me
that God is here, not commanding, judging, threaten-
ing, or punishing, but creating a world so wonderful, a
prayer so obvious that could I but cease in my fever of
petition, I could witness its beauty, too.

THE LONG WALK HOME

Out walking one morning I saw a medium-sized turtle begin the dangerous journey across the road from one side of Monponsett Pond to the other. The traffic is pretty heavy, even at 6 a.m., and as the turtle left the safety of the roadside grasses, I looked right and could see a line of cars coming, led by a Harley-Davidson ridden by a leather-clad figure in a tinted Plexiglas helmet. The turtle was almost at the halfway point, destined for extinction beneath those burning wheels. I moved a few paces into the road and simply pointed to the turtle. The motorcyclist slowed, bringing his gleaming bike to a stop. He put out his arm to indicate to the cars behind him that they should not overtake. He allowed the turtle to cross in safety. Then he and I signaled a greeting to each other and went on our ways.

The turtle, the motorcyclist, and I were on different journeys that day, and mine was a journey of discovery. I discovered that compassion sometimes wears a motorcycle helmet. I found the place inside me that fears bikers and I made a few corrections. I don't know what kind of day the turtle had, or the person on the motorcycle, but my day was better for having encountered them.

THE WEDDING

I stand before two men who are facing each other.

Their hands are clasped as if in a traditional handshake. They are speaking to one another.

They say, "You are the life that brings me life. From the moment of our first meeting, I knew that God had brought us together."

They choke on the words, their faces are wet, but their hands are clasped and the words come.

I look from one to the other.

I watch their eyes, their mouths, their hands.

I am in the presence of the holy.

I tell the people, "This union is blessed by God; I do pronounce these men partners in life."

And then, they kiss.

THERE HAVE BEEN SEPTEMBERS

Whatever September means to you, bring it here and let it find its place in your belonging.

Those of you who dressed your child for the first day of school this week, welcome to September. You who readied the summer cottage for winter, welcome to September. You who tidied your desk, brought in the hanging plants off the porch, resealed your driveway, met a whole new class of children, welcome to September.

Those of you whose memories of summer will be smoothed onto the pages of a photograph album; those whose memories will line your forehead, or tear your heart, welcome to September. Those who carried a school bag for the first time, loved someone, said goodbye, cried some, cried a lot, welcome to September.

September has marked the best and the worst of times for me; there were new beginnings: my sister's birthday, my wedding day. But September makes me nostalgic, it's the smell of school and shyness, and the memory of a friend who died, and the way my clothes don't fit. And worry about the year ahead.

Thank you, September, for bringing us all together, to smile at each other, hug maybe, touch hands, join voices once again. Hang around awhile, give us warm autumn afternoons before we have to shake our sweaters out of their summer hiding, or mend the broken zipper on the windproof jacket.

Spirit of love and reunion, bless our house and our hours together; help us to feel the possibility of joy in this place, and friendship, and beginnings.

MONPONSETT POND TAKES TO THE AIR

There were small pools of water on the road, a mist in the air that smelled of October, and the possibility of a cool refreshing sleep after August's sweaty nightmares.

There is a hedge of evergreen bushes along the path of my morning walk, shaved close and perfect with smooth velvet tops like sofa cushions. But overnight, out of the top of one of the bushes had sprung two laughing columbine shoots, waving and dancing two feet above their host in reckless defiance of the gardener's enforced symmetry. "Not so loud," I wanted to warn them. "If you draw attention to yourselves, he will set about you with his shears." But the trim youthful shoots didn't care, and merely shrugged as I passed by.

The lake was the color of smoke and the heron gathered itself for flight, its wingtips sweeping the surface. I imagined how that sweet, cool dipping would feel to the furthermost tips of the long grey wings, a prayer to the spirit of the west. The heron and the lake were the exact same color, as if the lake had gathered itself for flight and formed the bird from its own elements.

Dare we rise reckless above the crowd, breaking up uniformity, challenging those who insist on straight lines and 90 degree angles? Dare we pull away from the surface, blending color and form in a new pattern? Spirit of life, open our eyes, that each morning will bring us its fresh surprise.

AS THE CROW FLIES

A crow is said to fly in a straight line from point of departure to destination, but that is not what I see. Crows fly in sweeping circular arcs across the apron of the sky, using all the available space from horizon to horizon before settling on the top swaying branch of the tallest tree.

You may think crows caw, that their voices are harsh. But I tell you a crow can whisper to its mate across a density of pines, and its voice is comfortable and reassuring. A crow is mighty in its passion, voracious in its appetite, and fearless in its flight. So I aspire to live as the crow flies and stretch my soul to meet the sky.

INVOCATION

The goddess beat sheets of rain at our doors last night, calling us to join her in the fullness of her flood, but this morning she had swept the sky carefully, leaving a few wisps of cloud so we shouldn't be engulfed by the blueness and made mad by the desire to fly. I stretch up my hands and imagine I can gather the strands of cloud and make a blossom of them.

A cluster of ducks swims on the cranberry bog, flooded and red with floating berries, while the priestly birches sway as if to mark the second canonical hour. Morning comes with magic in her basket and we are invited to partake.

MEDITATION ON ALL SOULS

Who are my people, where are you who birthed me to play in summer's circle? I think I see you out of the corner of my eye, gone before I can look again, working, talking, engaged, and alive.

My ancestors are all about me in the ragged edges of memory, like partially developed film; the details are sketchy now. No princes and ladies among them, but scullery maids and journeymen. I know their faces, but not their voices, not the way their clothes smell, not the soft hands warm and red from a day of washing sheets. Did they smile at me? Did they notice the little gifts I brought? I don't remember.

Bits of pieces of my people remain in memory's attic, hardly enough to make a tribe. Forebears in small brick cottages with sooty chimneys and outdoor toilets. Women with wrap-around aprons and men with cloth caps. Brown teapots and doilies and unheated bedrooms. My grandmother's slippers, my mother's bone-handled hairbrush. Just memories, without the power to haunt.

So I seek a new tribe, other meanings. The little girl at the shelter shows me a toy, her creased fingers cannot yet turn a key, but there is still strength in her hand as it touches mine. Though she doesn't know my name, she would come with me if I would make her toy work and protect her from a world that has roughened her skin, bruised her heart, and given her only broken toys. She is a needy child; therefore, is she not my child?

The old man who hardly knows me says he loves me because I bring him a bowl of food and sit there while he eats it. He is a hungry old man; therefore, is he not my father?

At home I listen to a tape of sacred music and I weep in my chair, and I cannot say if I weep for the child in the shelter or for the child I used to be. The spirits have no power to haunt, I claim, so why do I weep in nostalgia and regret my forgetfulness?

I look at the faces around a meeting table, across the sanctuary, in the candlelight of a meditation group, and I think: these are my people now; we belong to each other, I pour out my soul in trust to a new tribe. These are my people, who touch my hands, who invite me to come along, who make room for me to sit in the shadow of the candlelight and listen to their songs.

THANKS TO THE FRIENDLY, FAMILIAR

I went to the beach, and rested there, intent on prayer. For my soul was heavy and I had things I wanted God to hear.

But some flighty flock kept interrupting my thoughts. I don't know the make of bird but there were a lot of them, hanging off the bare branches of the birch trees, twittering with ferocious excitement. I knew they were getting ready to leave, and at once I wanted to be with them, flying in that geometric formation, right in the middle of the flock, able to look right and left and see only familiar shapes and hear friendly voices.

But I am too heavy. One of my thoughts weighed more than several of those birds together. So they flew in formation, cutting an arc across the face of the morning and were gone. And I was alone.

I closed my eyes and there was no discernible sound, except a hum of traffic perhaps a mile away. The ocean doesn't sing, the sky makes no sound, the earth doesn't creak in its daily round. Solitude is no symphony, and I felt that I belonged not to the sand nor the sea nor the sky, but only to the quiet.

Then, I was shaken by a familiar discordant voice: a gull flying overhead, hanging in space, who wasn't going anywhere. The voice of the gull was the sweetest note I had ever heard.

Thank God for the gulls who are not afraid of the storm, who do not leave when winter comes.

THE TEXTURE OF A POEM

Somewhere above me,
a meditation forms,
vague, misty, and vaporous.

My thoughts are tangled and disorderly,
waiting for the artisan in me to guide them,
brush them into coherent sentences until they shine:

It is winter again.
The snow weighs down the branches of the
    douglas pine
and the bird feeder ruffles the depth of white.

VALENTINE

Creation gives us snow.

Lest we imagine beauty was only for summer, or trees for leafing; just in case we thought cold was for winter or, at best, firesides or pots of pea soup, creation gives us snow.

Creation outlines each slender twig with snow, a flake at a time. With divine patience, winter writes a character, a syllable, a word, until nature's grace is there on every tenacious surface.

And what of you and me? Ought we to think we can do better in our building of trust that we dare hurry such a thing as friendship?

Let us write our vows slowly, knowing some of the words like snowflakes will fall away, that from time to time a misunderstanding will come like a gust of wind or a bird's foot to a snow-covered branch, disrupting the careful gifts of love. Let us work on our manuscript, mirroring nature's patience, until the love is whole and the drift of our days is done.

POLAR VISION

I went to the beach on the night of the full moon. I am accustomed to walking on this slip of sand at all seasons and all hours. Here I meet the Muse. She reaches into my dreams, calls out of me the ghosts of my history, and with them shapes my future.

This night there were cold, moon-cast shadows and slabs of blue ice, braced one against the other, spread across the beach. This was a landscape I'd never seen, a wind-whipped, winter-sculptured world, a temporary ice-made rock formation along my slim, smooth straight of sand.

I tried to walk forward and my shoes slid beneath me over the sheer face of these frozen chunks. Strange and graceless was my body, sliding about in a dance without rhythm or choreography. But there was something connected too, something I could only understand with the instinctively animal part of me that braced its muscles against the wind. That part of me belonged on the rocks of ice that night, the part that didn't mind the wind stiffening my face and hands.

I wanted in that moment to be covered with coarse hair and to turn my long wolf nose to the moon and howl out my being. Or to race on all fours across those frozen slopes, with fresh snow dusting and whitening my polar fur. But I am dependent upon clothes to keep my blood from freezing, and I am ill-suited for survival in this hard-edged landscape.

We live with the illusion that we are able to shape our lives, and make them fit a pattern that we have chosen. Rather, our lives are shaped by a rhythm and a creation so vast and beautiful that the greatest force of human ingenuity can barely glimpse it.

Take some time to get ice cold this winter, out there in some frozen waste of a back lot or beach, or a forest with white branches dipped in homage to the season. Feel the clarity of thoughts sharpened by a blast of truth from winter's wind. Look up, look down, and feel the throb of your heart, warm and beating. Let go of all illusion, and be at peace.

OURS IS A STORY OF FAITH

I hadn't walked in the mornings for weeks, not since the snow started. So I walked into the wind and it numbed my cheeks and forehead, and I leaned against it and addressed my questions to the silver winter sun softening the ice on Monponsett Pond. What happened? Why am I so often sad and disappointed in myself? How come love has its dark side and feelings hurt and truth isn't kind? Where is hope, to whom shall I turn, what is faith? What shall I tell them, I said to the torn clouds, what shall I tell these good people who struggle as I do and fail just as often?

And it seemed that the soft silver sun and the sound of the wind said, speak the truth, simply, speak your truth.

And so I say ours is a story of faith and hope and love. I say it is our need for one another that binds us together, that brings us limping and laughing into relationships and keeps us at it when we otherwise might despair at the fix we are in. I say it is the holy we need, the eternal beyond our comprehension, and one place we can find it is here, working and worshipping together. And I say there is a transcendent value worthy of our loyalty, upon which we may set our hearts, and its divine manifestation is love.

NOVEMBER MORNING

There was a snow goose this morning, and a crescent moon still visible through the freshly revealed branches of the maple, so recently leafed in yellow. The goose flies with its strong neck stretched out, and its broad wings lifting it powerfully over the restless waves. The red dawn braces over the horizon, and my crows wail that winter is coming.

And the lone wild bird flies on, never knowing that across the bay lives a man with a rifle, who shoots ducks for sport and leaves them to die in the water. Or perhaps the bird knows and flies on; perhaps the bird knows what we know, that the world is a place of beauty, and of madness, of violence, and of compassion. Perhaps the spirit that moves the bird to flight also moves in us to commit love in response to anger, and kindness where there has been killing.

I believe that love will prevail and peace will rule the earth only when we can bring ourselves to be fully, openly present to the pain that violence causes, when we know in the deepest, most truthful place in ourselves that each act of hatred tears at the fine web of life to which we are all attached, and must be countered by acts of healing. When we dare to feel another's pain, we shall be so deeply affected that we will not turn aside, but rush to be healers, lovers, friends.

SHADOWS OF UNKNOWING

Grey, the color of the lake before sunrise; grey, the underside of the gull that flies overhead while the earth blindly searches for morning.

Give me grey. Grey the color of not sure, don't know yet. Grey the color of compromise, maybe, let me think about it; grey for talking things over, listening again, thinking some more. Grey for the shaded areas of the other point of view, for the possibility of change. Grey for the smudged edges of what once was dogma, and now is doubt. Grey.

In the bright red and green, and blue and gold of the season, and the noise and the festivity, give me grey, for the quiet of my soul, the moment of heaviness before sleep, the peace of meditation.

The steel grey of the lake mirrors the grey clouds overhead, and the bird meanders through the grace of morning flight, waiting, watching the movement of a grey walker watching him. The earth bows to find the dawn and feels its first slanting beams.

Can I take this as a promise, I wonder. That after the questions, the doubts, and the hours of contemplation, there will be gold through the grey, promise fulfilled and truth revealed. I don't know, but I believe in small epiphanies, a single beam of light in the darkness, some sought-for star, some one certainty emerging from the grey. Meanwhile, let us embrace the doubt and cherish our unknowing and patiently await the dawn.

GRATITUDE IS NOT ENOUGH

The world is full of blessings: I have a home, a family, good fortune, good health. I have a job, a wonderful church family, and people whom I admire and respect to share my work.

I have a place to go with my weight of disappointment and water to bathe my hurts. I have the vision of sunrise over the ocean every day, and gulls whose voices chorus my song, a choir of chanting whenever I want it. I have memories.

I have a heart for breaking, and a melting fire in my blood to fracture my sanity and cause me to lie on the floor and cry to see children hungry, children dealing drugs, and children watching violence on television and in their homes. I have a pillow to catch my tears, voiceless trees to monitor my coming and going, and the wind to sing the requiem.

I have politicians in white shirts and striped ties to keep guns in the hands of boys in blue jeans and t-shirts. I have drug lords in Cadillacs to keep crack babies in slums. I have poetry and ocean to remind me of the Goddess, and the Goddess to remind me of AIDS and prejudice.

Well, I refuse to lie down and be good. I will not heal up neatly, sutures in a row, no scars. No I will not. I will shout out that I am here and hurting and I will demand of life that it return my shout decibel for decibel. I will speak of justice and kindness and beauty and truth, and I will try bravery though I am a coward, and I will honor wisdom though I am a fool.

I will find other broken people with divinity shining through their pain, to remind me that the human spirit is hard to defeat, that the world is young yet and we are just an idea; that love is not for ever, but a little love once in a while is worth the risk of keeping the door of our hearts wide open. And I look for goodness and know it when I see it, and I see it in you and your children and your dreams. And I can never be grateful enough.

EXPECT LIFE!

Do not live too far in the past or the future. Live now.

In each moment expect a miracle: ten kinds of birds at the feeder, and the tracks of a fox in the snow.

Pick up a magnifying glass and scrutinize that crocus. See the pollen at the center of the daffodil, life's dust, death-defying life. Be astonished at the flower, arrested by its beauty.

Run naked through the garden early in the morning and hope the wild geese fly by.

Get silly and laugh loudly with your grandchildren or your grandparents. Refuse to leave the dead behind, but bring their memory to all your chores and games and corners of quiet, warm tears.

Know always that joy and sorrow are woven together; one cannot be without the other. If you love, know that sometimes your love will bring you tears; if you grieve, know it is because at some time you were willing to love.

Do not be afraid to die today. But expect life!

NOW WINTER COMES

Now winter comes, its labored breath misting the morning, frost sparkling on the pier. Exposed now, the birds make no pretense of shyness, smothering the feeders, fueling against the cold.

In March I didn't welcome spring's celebration, exploding from every limb's end; but today I am not ready to batten down for winter. Give me another morning to stand coatless before the awakening dawn.

But pine boughs have already been wreathed and bowed, and fir trees cut and limbed for countless living rooms. So let me breathe good fresh air and wrap my coat around me.

And let our hearts warm to smells and smiles of winter. Let us hold hands against the cold and sing carols to the season winter with merriment. And with hopeful hearts, let Christmas be received.

Soltice

LEGACY

Maybe love does not die, is not obliterated by hurts or anger. Maybe love does not dissipate, or sink like silt to dry out in the sun. Maybe love is not wasted or silly, or found to be something other than love.

Perhaps the love that settled about our shoulders and caressed us for a spell was created by ancient lovers from Sumer and Pompeii, blown by the winds around the south China sea, gathering strength across continents and through centuries. When we let go of it, perhaps it floated on, embracing other strangers unexpectedly, who turn toward each other, seeing the other for the first time, changed by the cloud of love that has gathered them together. Oh, my dear, do not despair that love has come and gone. Although we are broken, the love that spilled out of us has joined the love that circles the world and makes it blessed.

UNITARIAN UNIVERSALIST
MEDITATION MANUALS

This list includes all meditation manuals since the merger in 1961. For information about meditations prior to 1961, contact Skinner House Books, 25 Beacon Street, Boston, MA 02108.